7 June to 19 August 1944
THE B...
OF NOR...

Text by Georges Bernage

American Translation by P.L. Jutras

Cover Photo : IWM. Model by L. Verret

HEIMDAL GUIDE

7 June 1944. On the previous day, the Normandy Beach Landings had been successful. Most everything had gone according to plan. To the West, in the American sector, the 82nd and the 101st US Airborne Divisions suffered a great number of casualties ; some paratroopers drowned in the flooded areas ; but, all in all, the mission was accomplished, generally speaking.

• The 4th US Infantry Division had landed at Utah Beach without too much difficulty. On the other hand, it was a different story at « Bloody Omaha » where men were slaughtered on the shore and were unable to get a toe-hold on land. The landing operation almost failed, but the Americans, nevertheless, succeeded. The 2nd Bn. of the US Rangers took la Pointe du Hoc. In the British sector the beach landings, though difficult, were successful. In the Ran-

ville sector, paratroopers of the 6th British Airborne Division captured the bridge spanning the Orne River. D-Day objectives were almost reached, with one exception ; the city of Caen was not taken.

The Germans were overwhelmed ; they lacked the necessary materiel and supplies. Their air power was practically nil in the Western sector and, air power will seal the fate of the Battle of Normandy. They will have to call upon replacements who will be machine-gunned before reaching the front in Normandy.

On the morning of 7 June, it was safe to say that the beach landings had been successful but the Battle of Normandy, which will last for two and one half months, is just beginning. What is given here is a day to day report on this campaign : The Normandy Campaign.

1

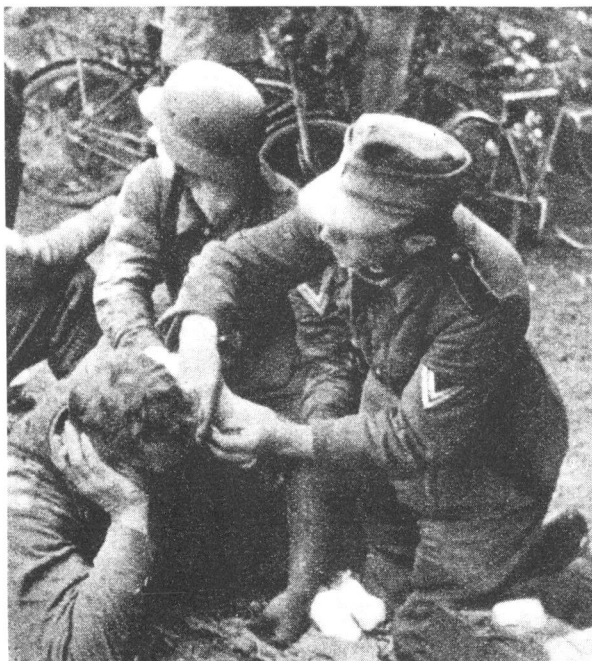

7 JUNE 1944 - In the British sector, the Germans will try to push the Allies back to the sea. They have but remnants of the 716th Inf. Div. and of the 21st Panzerdivision. But the British and Canadian paratroopers of the 6th Abn. Div. hold out in the Ranville sector. The 3rd British Inf. Div. will check and push back the advance elements of the 21st Panzerdivision.

In the Ranville sector on 7 June, two German NCOs render first aid to a wounded British paratrooper (above). Below : A captured Sergeant and a Corporal with two other paratroopers of the 6th British Abn. Div. (Coll. Heimdal).

This tank of the 21st Panzer, equipped with a PAK 40 anti-tank gun, is passing by the wing of a wrecked Horsa glider. (Bundesarchiv).

8 June. *Men of the 2nd US Ranger Bn. (on the opposite page above) have mopped up la Pointe du Hoc while US paratroopers (on the oppposite page and juste above) patrol Sainte-Mère-Eglise. (US Army photos).*

Above : GI's of the 8th Inf. Regt. of the 4th US Inf. Div. wading in the flooded fields between Utah Beach and Sainte-Mère-Eglise ; they reinforced the bridgehead in the Cotentin Peninsula. Paratroopers of the 101st US Abn. Div. are seen on the following page after the fall of Carentan on 12 June (US Army photos).

9 June — Harried and buzzed continuously by Allied aviation, the Germans could not muster more than three armoured divisions to the North and West of Caen (21st Pz-Div., 12th SS Pz-Div., Pz-Lehr). All concentration of German forces are crushed by naval artillery and particularly by Allied aviation. In the meantime the Allied Command was successful in landing a great number of forces ; the Canadians and British have landed 10 divisions, the Americans, 8 divisions. The fate of the Normandy campaign is already sealed. Allied victory is now assured but it will be very costly and long. Each yard of ground will be contested by a determined enemy familiar with the terrain. **On 12 June,** US paratroopers take Carentan.

Above : a Sherman of the 50th British Inf. Div. speeding along the highway South of Bayeux bypassing a wrecked Panzer IV type H German tank. This tank belonged to the 130th Regiment of the Pz-Lehr brought in to counter-attack. (IWM).

13 June, the British and Canadians were stopped in front of Caen by the determined resistance of the « Hitlerjugend » Division. The attack in this sector will be directed toward Tilly-sur-Seulles and will begin on 10 June.

Opposite : on 14 June near Lingèvres, British infantrymen of the « Durham Light Infantry » (50th Inf. Div.) have taken a few German prisoners. An English soldier is rendering first aid to one of the wounded German soldiers. (IWM).

8

To carry out the Allied offensive necessitates the solving of important logistical problems and gargantuan reinforcements in men, materiel and munitions. The artificial port of Arromanches, operational from 10 June, will be a vital supply artery. Notice the two sights of this port. (IWM).

On **13 June,** the Panzer-Lehr-Division, defending the Lingèvres and Tilly sector, is stopped head on by the 49th and 50th British Inf. Divisions. On the same date, the 7th British Armoured Division, « The Desert Rats », tries to pass round the German front but suffers heavy casualties at Villers-Bocage where it is attacked by the heavy tanks of Michael Wittmann. The Desert Rats were defeated. The British offensive will continue to mark time in front of Caen and Tilly.

On 21 June, an American column is going through Montebourg in ruins ; the offensive toward the major port of Cherbourg is carried out (US Army).

---

17 to 24 June. A terrible solstice storm will rage from 17 to 22 June in the English Channel. It will destroy the American artificial port, Mulberry « A », at Saint-Laurent (Omaha Beach) while Mulberry « B », at Arromanches, although damaged, will be repaired. The first V-1 « Buzz Bombs » begin to fall on the city of London as of 15 June : will this « Secret Weapon » change the course of the war ?

This storm will paralyse the British front for Lack of POL (petrol oil an lubricants) and munitions. Meanwhile, the American troops will continue their advance in the Cotentin. After having taken Saint-Sauveur-le-Vicomte, they will cut off the peninsula on 18 June at Barneville. They will take Valognes on the 19th of June and reach Fortress Cherbourg on the 21st. The Battle of the Val-de-Saire has now begun.

These photos taken on 24 June show the aftermath of the storm at the artificial port of Arromanches. Above : a floating causeway is twisted by the waves of a raging sea. Below : dislocated elements thrown on the coast. (IWM).

Verson, 25 June, these German grenadiers of the « Hitlerjugend » will face the British assault : the soldier in the foreground is carrying the well known MG 42 (machine-gun) Notice the camouflage uniforms. (coll. Heimdal).

25 June, near Verson (West of Caen) young grenadiers of the 12th SS Pz-Div. « Hitlerjugend ». They are wearing camouflage jackets and they have darkened their faces. (Coll. Heimdal).

25 JUNE - The British front begins to move after the Battle of Tilly which ended on 18 June, and after the interlude caused by the storm. The bloody battle of the Odon River (Operation Epsom) begins on the 25th of June. The determined adversaries of this British offensive will be these young grenadiers of the « Hitlerjugend » division. They will be killed on the spot.

End of June, German soldiers an FM squad, of the 16th Luftwaffen-Felddivision patrolling Place Courtonne at Caen (above). (Bundesarchiv). Below : West of Caen, a Panther tank on its way to affront Allied tanks. (Coll. Landrien).

Fontenay-le-Pesnel is taken by the British. But the « Panzers » of the Ist SS Panzer Korps control the heights of Rauray. The British send 60.000 men into the battle (an armoured division, two independent armoured brigades, in all 600 tanks). On **26 June,** the 15th Scottish Inf. Div. is backed up by Churchill tanks of the 31st Armoured Brigade. Cheux and Manvieu will be taken from the Germans, but the offensive is stopped South of Cheux. On 27 June, the British 49th Inf. Div. will finally take Rauray. The Scots will form a corridor of 10 kilometers in depth in the German front.

Below : 26 June, Operation « Epsom » is kept up ; these British infantrymen are firing upon German positions from the edge of town which is their departure base. They are supported by the fire of a Bren machine-gun (IWM).

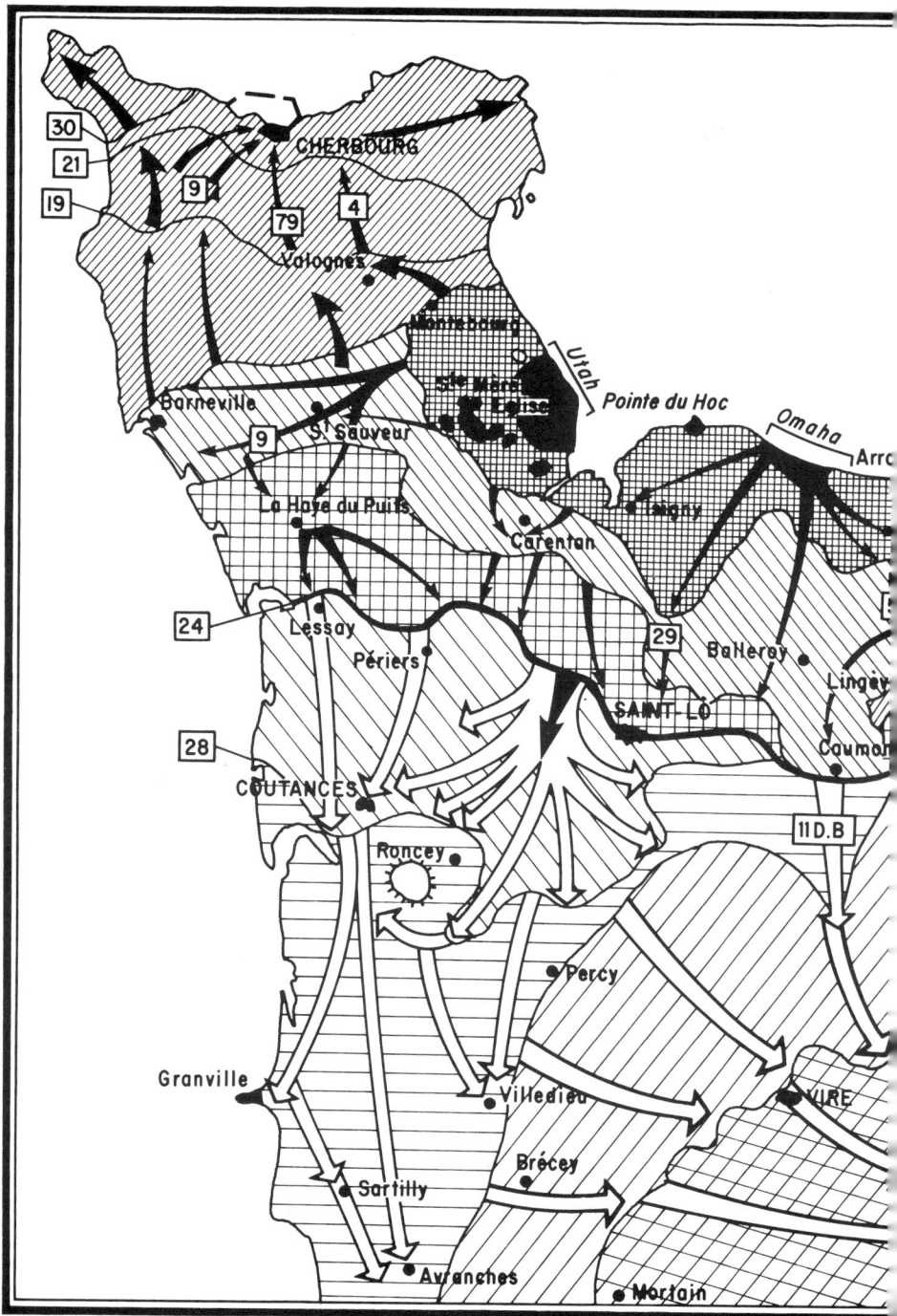

30
21
19

CHERBOURG

9

79

4

Valognes

Utah

Montebourg

Ste Mère Eglise

Pointe du Hoc

Omaha

Arro

Barneville

9

St Sauveur

La Haye du Puits

Carentan

Isigny

24

Lessay

Périers

29

Balleroy

Lingay

SAINT-LO

Caumon

28

COUTANCES

Roncey

11 D.B

Percy

Granville

Villedieu

VIRE

Brécey

Sartilly

Avranches

Mortain

Until 24 July, the Allies will advance very slowly. On the 25th of July (Operation Cobra-General Omar Bradley) the Americans will break through the German front, thus enabling the encirclement of German units in the « Falaise Pocket » on 19 August.

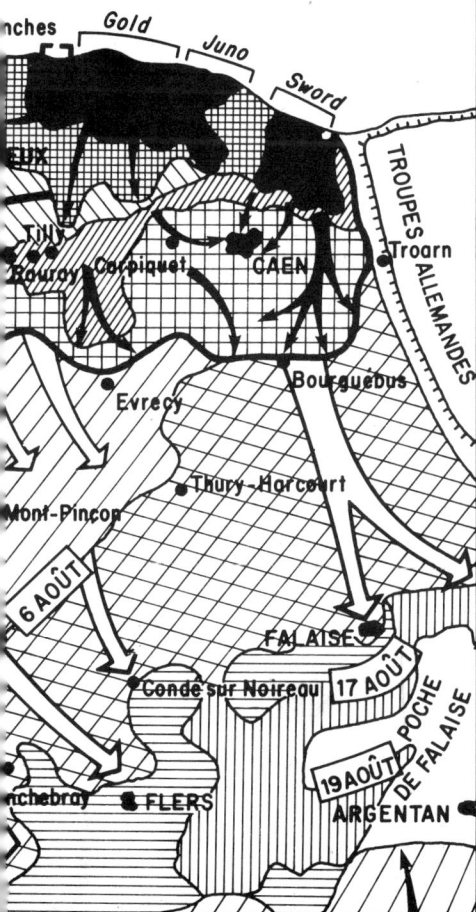

Front 6 June evening
Front le 6 Juin au soir

Front 10 June
Front le 10 Juin

Front 18 June
Front le 18 Juin

Front 30 June
Front le 30 Juin

Front 24 July
Front le 24 Juillet

Front 28 July
Front le 28 Juillet

Front 30 July
Front le 30 Juillet

Front 6 August
Front le 6 Août

Front 16 August
Front le 16 Août

Front 17 August
Front le 17 Août

Front 19 August
Front le 19 Août

Poche allemande
German pocket

Gold
Juno
Sword

nches

TROUPES ALLEMANDES

Tilly
Bouray Carpiquet
CAEN
Troarn

Bourguébus

Evrecy

Thury-Harcourt

Mont-Pincon

6 AOÛT

FALAISE

Condé sur Noireau
17 AOÛT
POCHE DE FALAISE

19 AOÛT

nchebray FLERS
ARGENTAN

(Carte G. BERNAGE)

26 June - Battle of the Odon River. Above : men of the 6th « Royal Scot Fusiliers » hovered by a smoke-screen, are ready for an attack with fixed bayonets. Below : a few hours later, some infantrymen are mopping up Saint-Manvieu : notice the belfry of the church in the background. These British soldiers are searching for isolated enemy snipers.

29 JUNE - The IInd SS Panzer Korps reinforces the sector with its two armoured divisions, the « Frundsberg » and the « Hohenstaufen » ; the British must repel heavy counter-attacks in the Bridgehead of the Odon River. The British are now on the defensive in this sector.

The Battle of the Odon. Above : 27 June, a wounded British soldier is carried to a « Universal Carrier » ambulance to be brought to the rear area. Below : 28 June, an isolated sniper of the « Hitlerjugend » captured near Rauray is brought in by soldiers of the 49th British Infantry Division. Rauray was a strong-point of German resistance. (IWM photos).

27 June — The first US Army has entered Cherbourg at 10 : 15 A.M. on the 26th of June following the combats to reach the entrenched enemy surrounding the city. 37.000 German soldiers are captured.

Opposite : one of the German soldiers belonging to a Schiffsstamm-abteilung (Fort du Roule Museum). Above : General Ira Wyche, Commander of the 79th US Inf. Div. with a few of his men at the summit of Fort du Roule on 27 June. (US Army).

Above : Caen in ruins on 9 July (IWM) Opposite : German soldiers of the 21st Panzer-Division in the Bavent forest, early July. (Heimdal).

4 to 9 July — One month after D-Day, Caen, which was to have been taken on D-Day, 6 June 1944, is still occupied by the Germans. This important Norman city, destroyed by repeated bombardments, will be taken by the Canadians who, after heavy fighting, take over Carpiquet on 4 July, then secure the city of Caen from the 4th to the 9th of July.

7 JULY — North of Saint-Lô, the Americans are hindered by the Norman bocage and advance yard by yard in front of a determined enemy who has the advantage of a well known terrain, and uses it fully. But, on 7 July, the 117th US Inf. Regt. crosses the Vire River at Airel on its way to Saint-Jean-de-Daye.

Above : 7 July, at Saint-Fromond, an American « M 10 Tank Destroyer » about to cross the Vire River on the bridge at Airel. Below : German soldiers killed on 7 July while defending Saint-Fromond. (US Army photos).

On 10 July, Caen is taken. Canadian and British soldiers watch over the city from the castle built by William the Conqueror who had conquered England in 1066... Above : a Corporal watching over Rue de Geole from the draw-bridge at the castle. Opposite : a P.I.A.T. team. (IWM photos).

9 JULY — At dawn, three Allied divisions take off to attack Caen from West to East : the 3rd Canadian Inf. Div., the 59th and 3rd British Inf. Divisions. They will be met grenadiers of the « Hitlerjugend » Pz.-Div.

Above : 15 July, near Hill 112, German mortars have destroyed this 17 pounder anti-tank gun and its tractor. Opposite : 16 July, East of Evrecy, an impenetrable spot, these men of the 4th « Royal Welsh Fusiliers » (53rd Inf. Div.) in a deep shelter for protection against continuous artillery and mortar shelling. (IWM).

10 July — From the 10th to the 19th of July, the British will storm Hill 112, a strategic point Southwest of Caen ferociously defended by the men of the IInd SS Panzer Korps. The taking of this sector would allow the British to enter Caen from the South.

Above : a Sherman bulldozer and men of the US 105th « Combat Engineer Bn. » on 8 July at the Airel bridge. Photo below (just above) Saint-Fromond on 11 July, an American column awaiting orders to attack. (US Army photos).

Above : the Battle of the Hedgerows, 18 July, near Lessay (US Army). Opposite page, above : in the Saint-Lô sector. Below : Saint-Lô in ruins is finally taken on 18 July. (US Army).

Meanwhile, the American army will try to get out of the Norman bocage in front of Saint-Lô and Lessay. It will take Saint-Lô on 18 July and will break out toward Marigny and Coutances after having crushed the « Panzer Lehr » sector with a carpet of bombs.

After the 25 July breakthrough, the Americans reached Avranches on the 30th of July. The German front is outflanked, the Americans emerge toward Brittany and Anjou. An encirclement movement is in the making. The Germans fail in their offensive on Avranches and will retreat progressively. The British will follow and the whole front will pivot from Bourguébus. Above : 26 July, the British are still observing at Maltot (notice R.T.R. Churchill tank) ; just above : 1st August, a Sherman tank speeds along on the highway near Beuvrigny. (IWM).

The Bocage breakthrough takes place from the 30th of July to the 6th of August. Outflanked on their left wing, bypassed by the Americans, the Germans will have to withdraw to avoid being encircled and the British troops will advance. Mont-Pinçon, an important strategic point, will be taken. The 11th Armoured Division will be in the middle of the advance. Above : on his way toward Vire, a dispatchrider is given a glass of cider. (IWM).

Above : on 2 August at Jurques, near a wrecked British gun, this « Tommy » is covering a street with his FM Bren ; many more small villages of the Bocage region will experience hard combats which slow down the battle. (IWM).

Near Juvigny, in the Mortain sector, these American infantrymen are still advancing slowly, while their comrades, more to the South, are charging down the Maine and Anjou regions in order to encircle the Germans in what will soon become the « Falaise Pocket ». (US Army).

From the 6th to the 19th of August — On the 7th of August, the Germans, having assembled what was left of their armoured units, counter-attack at Mortain. They want to stop the american breakthrough. But they are crushed by Allied fighter-bombers and fail. They must now retreat to avoid encirclement.

On 16 August, a pocket from Falaise to Carrouges in passing through Flers contains many German units, the remnants of the German 7th Army, fighting during their retreat. But everything will be precipitated. On 17 August, the Americans, to the South are already at Bourg Saint-Leonard while the British are at

Above : 10 August, the British advance, but isolated German snipers are dangerous, British squads take off to flush them out (above). One of them has been captured (below) ; he is an SS Waffen who is wearing an American camouflage outfit, unless this photo has been reconstituted... (IWM).

Falaise, a few kilometers to the North. The noose will close on the German forces assembled in a rather limited space. Allied aviation will dive in for the kill : it will be an apocalyptic carnage.

Conclusion :
As early as 7 June, the Germans having failed to « push the Allies back to the sea » the fate of the Battle of Normandy is settled. But a long war of attrition will follow during which the Allies will face harsh German resistance. The Germans will skillfully use their meager means of defense in Normandy.

On 25 July, the Americans break through the front between Saint-Lô and

Argentan after the battle, the church of Saint-Germain, rises above the ruins. This Norman city, destroyed like many others, will have experienced the last engagements of the Falaise Pocket where this Panther tank was stopped. (IWM).

Périers, it is the onslaught ; the Battle of Normandy definitely lost by the Germans. During more than three weeks the battle will rage and a part of the German troops will be encircled in the « Falaise Pocket » (inexactly named by Eddy Florentin, « Stalingrad in Normandy ») ; the Germans will leave 10.000 dead in the Falaise Pocket along with 40.000 wounded and prisoners but will be able to evacuate 50.000 men. Other German troops installed along the Dives River will also retreat beyond the Seine River. But the Battle of Normandy is now over with and the Allies will be in Paris already on 25 August 1944.

G. BERNAGE

Georges Bernage éditeur — Achevé d'imprimer sur les presses de l'Imprimerie Alençonnaise
2e trimestre 1985 — N° d'ordre 3323